MW00987908

Backyard Trampolining

A Comprehensive Guide for the Trampolinist

Darlene Traviss

Illustrations by
Steve Grannary and Lorne Holman

Brush
Education Inc.

Brush Education Inc.
www.brusheducation.ca
contact@brusheducation.ca

Printed and manufactured in Canada

Library and Archives Canada Cataloguing in Publication
Backyard trampolining
Traviss, Darlene
Includes index.
ISBN 9781550590838
1. Trampolining—Handbooks, manuals, etc. I. Title
GV555.T72 1994 796.47 C94-910235-0

We acknowledge the financial support of the Government of Canada through the Canada Book Fund for our publishing activities.

 Canadian   Patrimoine
Heritage   canadien

This book is dedicated to Kurt and Erika and the many other backyard trampoline enthusiasts anxious to learn more about this exciting sport.

This book is also dedicated to my parents. Thank you for giving me the opportunity to participate in gymnastics and trampoline over the years. Without your support, this book would not have been possible.

Contents

Chapter 4 *Intermediate Skills & Combinations*

Chapter 5 *Advanced Skills & Combinations*

Introduction

Welcome to the fun and exciting world of backyard trampolining! Backyard trampolines are becoming a common piece of equipment in the yards of many families. When used in a safe manner, your backyard trampoline can provide you with hours of enjoyable recreation. To gain the full benefits of this exciting activity and to ensure that the risk of injury is minimized, you should read this book in its entirety.

The skills presented in Backyard Trampolining can take you from a beginner to an advanced level of trampolining. Regardless of how much or how little trampolining you have previously done, it would be wise to begin with the section "Important Basics" before advancing to beginner, intermediate and finally advanced skills and combinations. All skills are presented in an easy to follow format:

- Prerequisites for each skill are given. It is important to master the prerequisites before attempting a new skill.

- A written description of each skill is provided in easy to understand terms.

- Detailed diagrams accompany the written description to further simplify technique and illustrate body positions.

- Key points are listed to help eliminate the "trial and error" process.

- Progressions are given to further simplify learning.

- An Error Detection and correction chart is also presented with each skill as a quick reference for correcting common mistakes.

- Variations of skills and ways to improve technique are given for a challenge once the trampolinist has mastered the fundamental skill.

Disclaimer

The misuse of a backyard trampoline can be dangerous and may lead to injury. The intent of this book is to better educate individuals on the proper use of a backyard trampoline. This book is not a standard for all persons using a trampoline. Progress at your own pace and adhere to the following guidelines:

1. Ensure that your trampoline is properly assembled in a level area with at least 10 unobstructed feet (3 metres) on all sides and a minimum of 20 unobstructed feet (6 metres) above the trampoline bouncing surface. The area directly below the bouncing surface must be kept clear at all times.

2. Perform the Stop Bounce after every skill or sequence of skills, or whenever you deviate from the centre of the trampoline.

3. Never jump off a trampoline, always *climb* off.

4. Keep your bouncing low and under control. Consistently land in the centre of the trampoline.

5. Allow only one person on the trampoline at a time.

6. Do not leave children unsupervised on the trampoline.

7. Avoid bouncing for long periods of time and do not bounce when you are tired.

8. Do not use your backyard trampoline when under the influence of alcohol or drugs.

9. Ensure that spotters are always stationed around the trampoline.

10. Master the specified prerequisites before attempting a new skill.

11. Do not attempt back flips (back somersaults), multiple somersaults or twisting somersaults on your backyard trampoline.

Before You Start . . .

Buying Considerations

A trampoline is a major purchase. With several brands and styles to choose from it can be a confusing decision for any consumer. To get the best possible trampoline for the amount you are prepared to pay, you will want to consider things such as the size, shape and design of the trampoline, warranties and follow-up service.

Price

Different brands and styles of trampolines will vary in price. Generally you get what you pay for so be sure to read the sections on what to look for in the various components of the trampoline.

Decide who will be using your trampoline – adults, children or both. If trampoline use will be restricted to children under 80 lbs (36 kg) you may want to consider purchasing a child-size trampoline. Children's trampolines can range in size from 4'6" x 6' (1.4 m x 1.8 m) rectangular trampolines to 9' (3 m) round, octagon or twelve-sided trampolines. Child-size trampolines usually cost much less than the standard-size trampolines. It must be remembered that a child-size trampoline should only be used by small children and if adults or teens plan to use the trampoline, you should consider paying the additional amount for a larger trampoline.

Size and Shape

Consider the amount of space you have available in your yard. There is no point in buying a very large trampoline if you do not have an adequate amount of yard space.

Trampolines come in a variety of shapes and sizes. Rectangular trampolines can range in size from 4'6" x 6' to 9' x 16' (1.8 m x 5 m). All measurements are based on the outside perimeter of the frame. Octagon, 12-sided or similar variations of the circular shaped trampoline can range in diameter from 9' to 16'. Keep in mind, the larger the bouncing area, the less spring your trampoline will give you.

The rectangular-shaped trampoline has been around the longest and is still quite popular with many trampolining enthusiasts. Some rectangular trampolines provide more spring than variations of the round trampoline.

Round, 12-sided or 8-sided trampolines are safer for younger children with the outside frame always being an equal distance from the central bouncing area.

Whether you decide on a rectangular, circular, 8-sided or 12-sided trampoline, all styles have certain benefits and drawbacks. Quite often, the shape you choose is based on personal preference.

Frame

The frame is one of the most durable components of your trampoline. When comparing trampoline frames, look for a frame that has tight fitting pipes. Loosely fitted pipes can result in a break in the weld causing instability and increased wear on the springs and bed. Look for reinforcements in the frame: Double piping versus single piping, especially in areas receiving large amounts of stress. Ensure that the attachment points between the frame and the springs are durable and secure. One final consideration when comparing frames, some manufacturers will galvanize frames while others will paint their frames. Galvanizing is a process that retards rusting. Galvanized frames will weather much better than frames which have been painted.

Springs

Look for a trampoline that has galvanized springs to minimize rusting. Ensure that the hooked ends of your springs always point downward when assembling your trampoline. This will reduce the risk of snagging the trampoline pads, clothes or skin.

Pads

Trampoline pads are essential for safety. Pads should cover the springs and the trampoline frame. Trampoline pads will vary in quality. Some manufacturers use a carpet underlay or foam rubber. Over time, moisture will be absorbed by these less expensive materials and the pads will begin to deteriorate.

Ethafoam is another material used as a filling for trampoline pads. Ethafoam is a durable material that will not compress and absorbs very little water.

In addition to the material used inside your trampoline pads, consider the material used as an outer covering. Outdoor awning material is common for pad covers and has proven to be strong and relatively weather resistant. Inspect the attachments used to hold the pads onto the frame. Some manufactures will glue straps onto the pads while others will stitch ties or straps onto the pads. Stitching will generally wear better than glue.

Some pads attach to the trampoline frame with steel buckles or snaps which may rust over time. Look for pads that attach with a plastic or rust-resistant device.

Bed

It is important to choose a trampoline with a durable bed (bouncing surface). Rubber was the most common material used for trampoline beds in the seventies and early eighties. Rubber beds work well in warm weather but tend to shrink and become difficult to bounce on in colder weather. Rubber beds are solid and prevent light and moisture from passing through; this is a consideration if you have grass under your trampoline that you do not want to kill. In colder climates, trampolines with rubber beds should be taken down over the winter as snow accumulation may stretch the bed.

Many manufacturers now use polypropylene for trampoline beds. Polypropylene is a durable synthetic material used in ropes and fishing lines. Polypropylene beds will shrink and stretch marginally during temperature changes, thus maintaining a fairly consistent bounce throughout the year in all climates. Polypropylene trampoline beds allow light and moisture to pass through tiny holes in the material. Trampolines with polypropylene beds will not damage grass directly beneath the bouncing surface.

In addition to the type of material used for the trampoline bed, also consider the design of the bed. Look for a solid trampoline bed that does not have seams across the jumping surface. Seams directly exposed to the stresses of bouncing may give out over time.

Give consideration to how the trampoline bed is attached to the springs. Hoops or hooks can be sewn into the bed or clamped on. Attachments that are sewn in generally last longer than hooks that are clamped on.

Warranties and Follow-Up Service

Reputable trampoline manufacturers should provide warranties on the various parts in addition to accessible follow-up services. Before purchasing your trampoline you may want to ask the following questions:

• Does the trampoline cost include delivery and set-up?

• If the trampoline or a part of the trampoline needs repair, where must it be sent? Is the shipping covered under the warranty? How long does it take to repair certain trampoline parts?

• Are there separate warranties for the frame, the bed, the pads and the springs? Are there any conditions attached to the warranties?

Installation

Your trampoline should come with an Owner's Manual that outlines set up and take down procedures for the apparatus. There are other important considerations for set up and take down that may not be included in your manual.

Choosing a Location

Position your trampoline in an open area that extends outward a minimum of 10 feet (3 m) from the frame. The ground beneath the trampoline must be level. There should not be any overhead obstructions such as trees, roof overhangs, powerlines, etc. A minimum clearance of 20 feet (6 m) above the bouncing surface is necessary for safety.

Sinking your Trampoline

To further increase the safety of your trampoline, you may want to lower the apparatus to ground level by digging a hole with similar dimensions. This is an especially good set-up for younger children. Although the trampoline is at ground level, care must be taken when mounting and dismounting: *Never bounce off your trampoline*, always climb on and climb off.

15

Stabilizing Your Trampoline

Depending on how soft the ground is beneath your trampoline, you may experience some settling of the frame into the grass or soil. This settling could cause the trampoline to become lopsided and unstable. As a precautionary measure, place cement blocks beneath the supports of your trampoline. Wooden blocks a minimum of four inches (10 cm) thick will also work; plywood is not recommended as the force created by the trampolinist will split and break thin sheets of wood. Whether you decide to use wood or cement blocks, leave an outcrop of six inches (15 cm) around the supports as the trampoline will shift slightly. Be sure to check your bases periodically to ensure that the trampoline has not slipped off.

Safety Precautions

Safety precautions surrounding the use of your trampoline are very important. By following some set guidelines combined with common sense, the incidence of injury on your trampoline can be minimized.

Suggested Rules

1. Master the *Stop Bounce* before progressing to other skills. Perform the Stop Bounce after every skill or sequence of skills.

2. Always climb on and climb off your trampoline, *never jump off the apparatus.*

3. Keep your bouncing low and under control. Consistently land in the centre of the trampoline.

4. Allow only one person on the trampoline at a time.

5. Do not leave children unsupervised on the trampoline.

6. Avoid bouncing for long periods of time and do not bounce when you are tired.

7. Do not use your trampoline when under the influence of alcohol or drugs.

8. Ensure that *spotters* are always stationed around the trampoline.

9. Do not use your trampoline as a springing device to get onto other things.

10. Do not bounce in poor lighting or in the dark.

11. Progress at your own speed and use logical progressions. *Do not attempt a skill until you have mastered the necessary prerequisites and progressions.*

12. Do not attempt back flips (back somersaults), multiple somersaults or twisting somersaults on your backyard trampoline.

What to Wear

To prolong the life of your trampoline it is important to set certain attire requirements. Belt buckles, watches, shoes and other sharp objects or pieces of clothing should be avoided. Loose fitting clothing that allows for a wide range of motion is recommended. Long hair should be tied back.

Equipment on the Trampoline

Equipment should not be brought onto the trampoline. Balls, hoops, sticks and other toys or pieces of equipment can be very distracting for trampolinists and may damage the bed.

Flying Off

One of the biggest fears of trampoline owners is *flying off* (losing control and springing off the trampoline). Such a dismount can be very serious and potentially lead to injury. As previously mentioned, master the Stop Bounce and use the Stop Bounce whenever you move away from the centre of the bed.

Have people stand around the edge of the trampoline at ground level as *spotters*. If the person bouncing on the trampoline should ever come close to flying off, the spotters can push the trampolinist back toward the centre of the bed. Spotters should not attempt to catch a trampolinist who is out of control. Pushing the trampolinist back toward the centre requires less strength and is more effective than trying to catch the trampolinist.

If the centre of your trampoline is not clearly marked, paint an "X" in the centre. This mark will help trampolinists stay in the centre of the bed and reduce the potential for flying off.

Waivers

If neighborhood children and friends will be using your trampoline, you should consider having each participant, (or parent of the participant), sign a waiver.

18

The following waiver is only a sample. You may want to have a lawyer draw up a waiver as laws will vary depending on your province or state.

Sample Waiver

Participant's Name: _____

Emergency Contact: _____

Home Phone Number: _____

Trampoline activities, by their nature, involve certain elements of risk and involve a potential for bodily injury. I acknowledge this element of risk and agree to permit my child to use the trampoline at (your address). I understand that (your name), will not be held responsible should injury be incurred by the above named participant on the trampoline at the aforementioned location.

Signature of Parent or Legal Guardian _____

Signature of Trampoline Owner _____

Witness _____

Date _____

IMPORTANT BASICS

"ALTHOUGH TEMPTING, TOO HIGH AND HARD
A BOUNCE IS NOT RECOMMENDED..."

Warming Up

The importance of a warm up cannot be overemphasized. Warm-up stretches will not only reduce your risk of injury but they will also enable you to progress more effectively and reduce stiffness after your trampoline work out. The following exercises will stretch your major muscle groups. Hold each stretch for twenty to thirty seconds.

Neck Rotations

To stretch the muscles in your neck, drop your chin toward your chest and roll your head from side to side. It is not necessary to roll your head back as this can place an undue amount of strain on the joints and muscles of your neck. Half circles in the front will provide you with a good stretch.

Arm Circles

Slow, large arm circles will stretch the muscles in your shoulder region. Rotate your arms in both a forward and backward direction.

Side Stretches

Extend one arm over your head, place the other arm by your side. Slowly lean to one side, hold the stretch then reverse your arm position and lean toward the opposite side. To maintain stability, stand in a Straddle position with legs shoulder width apart and the knees bent. When you are holding this stretch, do not let your body arch back or pike forward.

Quad Stretch

To stretch your quadriceps, the muscles on the front of your legs, bend at the knee, grasp the front of your foot, and slowly pull your heel toward your seat. To increase the intensity of this stretch, lift the knee upward and back. Do not let your knee move out to the side on this stretch.

Hamstring and Calf Stretch

To stretch the muscles on the backs of your legs, face your trampoline with your hands on the frame. Place one foot in front of the other foot. Lean forward and press your back heel to the ground. Keep both feet pointed forward.

You may want to add additional stretches to your warm up depending on your flexibility and skill level. Whatever additional stretches you choose to do, remember to hold each stretch for twenty to thirty seconds.

Body Positions

All trampoline skills revolve around four body positions: The tuck, pike, straddle and layout. By varying the body position, you can increase or decrease the difficulty of a skill. Practice these positions while sitting.

Tuck

The tuck is performed by pulling the knees toward the chest and placing one hand on each shin. Keep your knees slightly apart in the tuck.

Pike

The pike is performed by extending the legs outward and reaching toward the toes while keeping the legs together and straight.

Straddle

The straddle is performed by extending the legs forward and apart. Reach toward your toes (or knees depending on your flexibility) while keeping your legs straight.

Layout

The layout is performed by keeping your body straight with the chest slightly hollowed and the back flat. Do not arch your back in the layout position.

The No-Bounce Method

One of the biggest myths about trampolining is that you need lots of height to successfully perform a skill. This is not true! This is not to say that you should not bounce on your trampoline. As you progress and begin to feel more comfortable performing a certain skill, you may want to add a small bounce at first then gradually increase the height of your bounce *ensuring that control is maintained*.

The No-Bounce Method is a safe and easy way to learn new skills and simply means you perform a skill without any lead-up bouncing. You may circle your arms to initiate some momentum but do not let your feet leave the trampoline bed before doing the skill. The No-Bounce Method will make learning new skills easier, safer and less intimidating. All skills covered in this book should be first tried using the No-Bounce Method.

I TELL YOU, I DISTINCTLY HEARD A "THUD."

BEGINNER SKILLS
& COMBINATIONS

OK, SO FAR SO GOOD. NOW...

Stop Bounce

The Stop Bounce is necessary for control and safety and should be performed after a skill or sequence of skills and whenever the trampolinist deviates from the centre of the bed. When done properly all movement should stop immediately when the Stop Bounce is performed.

Land with your legs shoulder width apart, knees slightly bent, arms at chest height and in front of your body, chest and stomach pulled in and head level.

Prerequisites

None

Key Points

- Always start and finish the skill in the centre of the trampoline.
- Do not look down when performing the Stop Bounce; focus on the edge of the trampoline.
- Keep your stomach, back and leg muscles tight.
- Arms should be in front of your body and at chest height.

Progressions

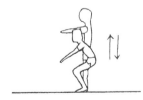

1. Stand in the centre of your trampoline and practice holding the Stop Bounce position with your arms in front of your body, feet shoulder width apart and the knees slightly bent. Slowly bend then extend at the knees to familiarize yourself with the movement

required to absorb and stop your bounce.

2. Perform the Stop Bounce with a small bounce.

3. Once you are able to stop after doing a small bounce, try the Stop Bounce after bouncing with more height.

For a Challenge

Have someone shout "Stop!" as you are bouncing and see how fast you are able to perform the Stop Bounce and come to a standstill.

Error Detection and Correction Chart

The Error Detection and Correction Charts will point out common mistakes made by trampolinists on various skills. At least one or two ways of correcting an error are presented. When referring to an Error Detection and Correction Chart for any of the skills covered in Backyard Trampolining, make only one correction at a time.

Error	Correction
your body continues to move after doing the Stop Bounce	– bend your knees to absorb and stop the bounce; do not bend past 90°
falling forward after doing the Stop Bounce	– focus on the edge of the trampoline; do not look down at your feet – keep your arms at chest height and in front of your body
falling backward after doing the Stop Bounce	– focus on the edge of the trampoline; do not look up or over your shoulder – keep your arms in front of your body, shoulder width apart and slightly below shoulder height – ensure that your body is slightly hunched over; do not arch your back or stick your stomach out

Basic Bounce

The Basic Bounce is one of the most important skills you will learn. This skill, when mastered, will make learning more advanced skills and combinations much easier and safer. It is important to maintain control on the Basic Bounce and consistently land in the centre of the trampoline bed.

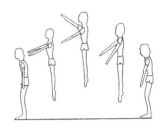

Lift your arms upward, keeping the elbows straight and the arms close together in front of your body. Stop at shoulder level and move your arms out to the sides, then back down to the starting position.

Prerequisites

Stop Bounce

Key Points

• Always start and finish the skill in the centre of the trampoline.

• Focus on the edge of the trampoline at all times.

• Keep your seat and stomach muscles tight.

• Do not make your arm circles too big at first.

Progressions

1. Using the No-Bounce Method, practise the arm movements for the Basic Bounce: arms start by your side, lift your arms up to chest level keeping the arms close together and in front of your body; the arms then move out to the sides and drop back down to the

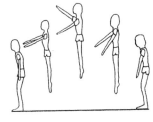

starting position in one fluid motion.

2. Starting in the centre of your trampoline, bounce without using your arms (keep your arms by your sides).

3. Now attempt some low bounces using small arm circles. When your body is in the air, your arms are up; when your feet make contact with the trampoline bed, your arms should be down and near your sides.

4. Bounce at a comfortable height, lifting the arms up through the centre on your ascent, stop at shoulder height and bring your arms down by your sides on the descent.

For a Challenge

Keep your legs straight and together in the air.

Extend your arms up to ear level on the ascent for maximum lift. Do not let your arms pass behind your head as this can throw you off balance.

Error Detection and Correction Chart

Error	Correction
falling backward or travelling backward and unable to remain in the centre of the trampoline bed	– keep your arms in front of your body and narrow on the ascent – make your arm circles smaller – do not allow your arms to pass behind your body at any point in the Basic Bounce – finish your arm circles at chest height – focus on the edge of the trampoline – maintain a flat back by keeping the seat and stomach muscles tight; do not arch your back – lower your bounce
falling forward or travelling forward when bouncing	– lower your bounce – keep your head level and focus on the edge of the trampoline; do not look down at your feet – make your arm circles smaller – ensure your arm circles are going in a backward direction
sore lower back	– maintain the pelvic tilt position by tightening stomach and seat muscles – keep your chest and stomach pulled in; do not arch your back – lower your bounce

Tuck, Pike and Straddle Jumps

Prerequisites

Stop Bounce, Basic Bounce, an understanding of the Basic Body positions.

Tuck Jump

The Tuck Jump is performed by bringing the knees toward the chest. Place one hand on each shin once your knees have reached chest level.

Key Points

- Always start and finish the skill in the centre of the trampoline.
- Focus on the edge of the trampoline.
- Keep the shoulders in an upright position.

Straddle Jump

The Straddle Jump is performed by bringing the legs up to a horizontal straddled position.

Key Points

- Always start and finish the skill in the centre of the trampoline.
- Focus on the edge of the trampoline.
- Keep your legs below horizontal until you feel more comfortable with the Straddle Jump.
- Keep your shoulders in an upright position.
- Reach forward for your knees or toes, depending on your flexibility.

Pike Jump

The Pike Jump is similar to the Straddle Jump, in that the trampolinist brings the legs up to a horizontal position in the air. Unlike the Straddle Jump however, the legs are held together for the Pike Jump.

Key Points

- Always start and finish the skill in the centre of the trampoline.

- Do not lean back in the Pike Jump; reach forward for your knees or toes and always keep your arms in front of your body.

- Focus on the edge of the trampoline.

Progressions

For Tuck, Pike and Straddle Jumps

1. Begin by using the No-Bounce Method for your Tuck, Pike or Straddle Jump.

2. Add a low bounce to the jump and finish with a Stop Bounce.

3. Bounce at a comfortable height before doing your Tuck, Pike or Straddle Jump and remember to finish with the Stop Bounce.

For a Challenge

Perform your jumps with good form: legs straight on the Straddle and Pike Jumps, legs together on the Tuck and Pike Jumps; legs horizontal on the Pike and Straddle Jumps.

Combine two or more jumps with only one bounce in between: Tuck Jump to feet, Pike Jump to feet, Straddle Jump to Stop Bounce. If you start to move away from the centre of the trampoline, do the Stop Bounce immediately.

Error Detection and Correction Chart

Error	Correction
falling forward in the air or on the landing	– lower your bounce – focus on the edge of the trampoline and do not drop your chin toward your chest – keep your legs lower and do not hold the Tuck, Pike or Straddle position as long – after touching your knees, shins or toes (depending on the skill), keep your arms in front of your body and at chest height for better balance
falling backward in the air or on the landing	– lower your bounce – look at the edge of the trampoline throughout the jump – tighten your back and seat muscles – do not allow your arms to pass behind your body at any point during the jump – do a Stop Bounce after your Tuck, Pike or Straddle Jump
unable to land on your feet after trying the jump	– do not hold the Tuck, Pike or Straddle position too long, touch your legs or toes then quickly bring your legs underneath you for the landing – lower your legs to below horizontal on the Pike and Straddle Jumps – bring your knees toward your chest on the Tuck Jump; do not bring your chest down to your knees – keep your shoulders, hips and feet in line on the take off and landing; do not lean forward or backward

Half Turn and Full Turn

The Half Turn and the Full Turn are important lead-up skills for several more advanced moves that involve twisting.

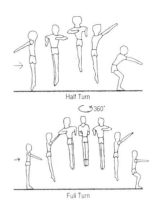

Half Turn

Full Turn

Prerequisites

Tuck Jump, Pike Jump, Straddle Jump

Key Points

- Always start and finish the skill in the centre of the trampoline.

- Master the Half Turn before attempting the Full Turn.

- Start by using the No-Bounce Method.

- Stand tall throughout the turn, do not let your body arch back or pike forward.

- Focus on the edge of the trampoline before and after the turn.

- Keep your arms in front of your body and at chest height after completing your turn.

Progressions

1. Start by using the No-Bounce Method for your Half Turn. Keep your body tight so that your head, torso and legs all twist at the same time. Initiate the turn by swinging your arms in the direction that you want to go. You do not need a large swing, especially for the Half Turn.

Pick something to focus on after the Half Turn. Immediately go into the Stop Bounce after you have spotted your focal point; this should stop your rotation.

2. Add a low bounce once you are able to do the Half Turn with no bounce. Remember to do the Stop Bounce after your turn.

3. Once you have mastered the Half Turn with a bounce, try a Full Turn. Start by using the No-Bounce Method. Pick a focal point and do a Stop Bounce after the Full Turn.

4. Add a bounce before doing your Full Turn and finish with the Stop Bounce.

Error Detection and Correction Chart

Error	Correction
unable to complete the Full or Half Turn	– do not drop your chin toward your chest; keep your head level throughout the turn – tighten up your body, especially your seat, stomach and back muscles – look hard and fast for a focal point, (a point behind you for the Half Turn or a point in front of you for the Full Turn), this will help initiate the rotation – bring your arms from an outstretched position to pulled in against your chest; when you pull your arms in, pull much harder and slightly across with your outside arm (if you twist to your right, pull your left arm across your body and toward your chest)
overtwisting the Half Turn or the Full Turn	– perform the Stop Bounce after doing a Half or Full Turn, your arms should finish in front of your body, outstretched and at chest height – look for a focal point; sometimes it helps to draw an "X" with a piece of chalk on one of the trampoline pads; once you spot your focal point, quickly do a Stop Bounce and finish with your arms open and at chest height – do not initiate the twist as quickly; instead wait a split second longer before looking for the focal point
falling forward during or after the Half Turn or the Full Turn	– lower your bounce or go back to the No-Bounce Method – keep your head level and focus on the edge of the trampoline; do not look directly down at the trampoline bed

Error Detection and Correction Chart (cont.)

falling forward during or after the Half Turn or the Full Turn (cont.)	– when in the Half or Full Turn, keep your arms at chest level (even when arms are pulled in); when you do your Stop Bounce, do not let your arms drop below chest height
falling backward during or after the turn	– keep your arms in front of your body throughout the turn – try to keep your shoulders, hips and feet in a straight line going into the turn, during the turn and at the end of the turn – lower your bounce or go back to the No-Bounce Method – do not arch your back
falling sideways during or after the Full Turn	– look harder for the focal point – keep your body tighter throughout the turn – do the Stop Bounce after the turn – lower your bounce or go back to the No-Bounce method – keep your arms at chest height during the twist
bouncing away from the centre of the trampoline bed in the turn	– lower your bounce until control is regained, then gradually add more height – do not initiate the turn too soon; wait until your feet have left the trampoline bed

For a Challenge

Keep your legs straight and together throughout the turn.

Try a 1½ or Double Turn. Follow the same progressions as you would for a Half or Full Turn.

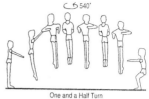

One and a Half Turn

Combine different jumps with the Full and Half Turn: Half Turn directly into a Pike Jump, Tuck Jump into a Half Turn into another Tuck Jump, Half Turn into a Straddle Jump into another Half Turn.

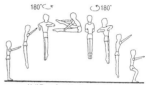

Half Turn, Straddle Jump, Half Turn

Invent your own jumps. Always take off with both feet at the same time and finish with the Stop Bounce.

Seat Drop

The Seat Drop is performed by going from your feet into a sitting position then rebounding back up to your feet.

Prerequisites

Tuck Jump, Pike Jump, Straddle Jump

Key Points

- Always start and finish the skill in the centre of the trampoline.
- Focus on the edge of the trampoline.
- Do not lean forward or backward. Keep your back straight and your shoulders level in the Seat Drop.
- Reach forward and upward to go from your seat back to your feet. Think of touching the trampoline then reaching for the sky.

Progressions

1. Sit on the trampoline in the Seat Drop position: back straight, knees straight, legs together, hands flat and by your sides, head level.
2. Using the No-Bounce Method, bend your knees so that you are closer to the trampoline bed and in one smooth motion, kick your feet out from under you and land in the Seat Drop position. Do not worry about rebounding back to your feet at this stage.
3. From standing and without a bounce, kick your feet out from under you, land in the Seat Drop

position then try to stand up by reaching forward and upward.

4. Try the Seat Drop with a low bounce and finish with the Stop Bounce.

For a Challenge

Do two or more Seat Drops in a row. Take only one bounce in between each Seat Drop. Remember to touch the trampoline bed then reach for the sky on each Seat Drop.

Error Detection and Correction Chart

Error	Correction
unable to drop down into the Seat Drop	– keep your shoulders and hips in line with your feet before going into the Seat Drop – do not lean backward or forward before doing the Seat Drop – extend your legs out further when dropping into the Seat Drop, never land with your legs crossed or bent underneath you – stretch out your hamstring muscles if you are having difficulty keeping your legs together and straight (see pages 23–24 for stretches)
falling backward after landing in the Seat Drop position	– ensure that your hands are flat on the trampoline bed and by your sides; never put your hands behind your body in the Seat Drop – keep your hips at a 90° angle and your back straight – focus on the edge of the trampoline – do not let your heels lift off the trampoline bed in the Seat Drop position
unable to get back to your feet after doing the Seat Drop	– place your hands by your sides on the Seat Drop; as soon as your body starts to rebound off the trampoline bed quickly lift your arms forward and up to ear level – keep your hips at a 90° angle, back straight and eyes focused on the edge of the trampoline when you are in the Seat Drop position – keep your body tighter

Hands and Knees Drop

The Hands and Knees Drop can be used as a lead-up skill for more advanced tricks such as the Stomach Drop, the Roller and the Cat Twist. The Hands and Knees Drop is a relatively simple skill to master after a bit of practice.

It is not recommended, however, that you perform the Knee Drop. Going down onto your knees without the support of your hands puts an undue amount of strain on the lower back and can cause whiplash.

Prerequisites

Seat Drop

Key Points

* Always start and finish the skill in the centre of the trampoline.

* Keep your back level in the Hands and Knees Drop position.

* Do not sit back on your heels, maintain a 90° angle behind the knees.

* Look forward, not down.

* Keep your elbows straight with your hands flat on the trampoline bed and the fingers pointing forward.

Progressions

1. Practice holding the Hands and Knees Drop position to familiarize yourself with how you will be landing in this skill.

2. Start in the Hands and Knees Drop position and attempt to bounce on your hands and knees by pressing down into the trampoline bed. This is a difficult step that takes a fair bit of practice to co-ordinate. Do not become discouraged if your backside starts "bucking up" before your torso! This progression will help develop co-ordination so that your hands and knees touch the bed at the same time in the Hands and Knees Drop.

3. Using the No-Bounce Method, lower your shoulders then drop into the hands and knees position. *Do not sit back on your heels!* Keep your seat up and maintain a 90° angle behind the knees.

4. From a low bounce, go into the Hands and Knees Drop then rebound back onto your feet.

Error Detection and Correction Chart

Error	Correction
sitting back on your heels	lower your shoulders going into the Hands and Knees Drop
your knees are hitting the trampoline bed before your hands	– keep your knees at a 90° angle in the Hands and Knees Drop position – lower your bounce or go back to the No-Bounce Method – lean forward in the hands and knees position so that your shoulders are directly above your hands
your hands are hitting the trampoline bed before your knees	– lower your hips and raise your shoulders – lower your bounce or go back to the No-Bounce method
having difficulty getting from the Hands and Knees position back to your feet	– tighten up your muscles, especially in the shoulders and back – lower your bounce – keep your arms straight in the Hands and Knees Drop, then push away from the trampoline as your body starts to rebound upward – focus on the edge of the trampoline, quickly bring your head and shoulders upward as your body rebounds off the trampoline bed

For a Challenge

Practice the Hands and Knees Drop with your legs together throughout the skill.

Try doing two or more Hands and Knees Drops in a row using only one bounce between each skill.

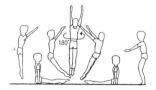

Swivel Hips

The Swivel Hips are performed by doing a Seat Drop facing in one direction, then immediately rebounding into a vertical Half Turn, followed by another Seat Drop facing in the opposite direction.

Prerequisites

Seat Drop, Half Turn, Full Turn

Key Points

- Always start and finish the skill in the centre of the trampoline.

- Begin and end the Swivel Hips using the proper Seat Drop position: Back straight, head level, legs straight and together and hands by your sides.

- A strong arm lift will help to give you height in between the Seat Drops and make the Half Turn easier to complete.

- Focus on a point behind you and look hard and fast for that focal point after your body has rebounded out of the first Seat Drop.

- Twist in the same direction. This is especially important when you start doing more than two Seat Drops in the Swivel Hips.

Progressions

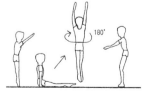

1. Seat Drop Half Turn to feet with a low bounce. Emphasize a strong narrow arm lift coming out of the Seat Drop and going into the Half Turn. Do not let your arms pass behind your body. Look hard and

fast for a focal point behind you to initiate the twist.

2. Half Turn into a Seat Drop using the No-Bounce Method. Concentrate on doing a good Half Turn with your arms lifting to ear level, the legs together and the body tight. Look for a focal point behind you then drop into the Seat Drop position by extending the legs outward. Rebound out of the Seat Drop position to finish on your feet.

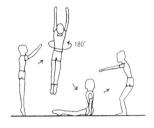

3. Seat Drop Half Turn to your feet, one bounce then drop into a second Seat Drop and finish on your feet.

4. Swivel Hips with a low bounce. Remember to perform a solid Seat Drop, lift with the arms going into the Half Turn and look for a focal point.

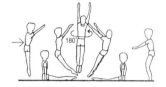

5. Swivel Hips with a regular bounce, finishing with the Stop Bounce.

For a Challenge

Do three or more Seat Drops in the Swivel Hips.

49

Error Detection and Correction Chart

Error	Correction
unable to complete the Half Turn	– as soon as your body starts to rebound out of the first Seat Drop, look hard and fast for a focal point behind you – keep your body tighter – stretch out your body in the Half Turn as it is harder to twist when your body is bent
unable to keep your legs straight	– stretch out your hamstrings – lift your arms upward as you rebound off your seat, this will give you more height and make it easier to keep your legs straight – you may be starting your Half Turn before you have rebounded out of the Seat Drop, wait until your body is almost vertical and your arms are above your head before initiating the turn
falling sideways in the first Seat Drop	– you may be starting your Half Turn before your body has started to rebound out of the first Seat Drop; ensure that your body is almost vertical and the arms are above your head before turning – keep your hands by your sides when you are in the Seat Drop Position on the trampoline bed
falling sideways in the second Seat Drop	– keep your back straight in the second Seat Drop – focus on the edge of the trampoline
falling backward in the Seat Drop	– place your hands flat on the trampoline bed on either side of your hips for stability when you are in the Seat Drop position – keep your heels on the trampoline bed when you are in the Seat Drop position – keep your back straight and your head level in the Seat Drop position – maintain a 90° angle at the hips in the Seat Drop position

Stomach Drop

The Stomach Drop is performed by dropping from your feet to your stomach then rebounding back up to your feet. It is important to remember that your stomach always lands where your feet used to be on the trampoline bed.

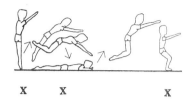

X   X   X

"X" marks the centre of the trampoline

Prerequisites

Hands and Knees Drop

Key Points

- Always start and finish the skill in the centre of the trampoline.

- Your stomach lands on the same spot that your feet used to be on.

- Keep your body tight, especially your seat, back and stomach muscles.

- All parts of your body touch the trampoline bed at the same time.

Progressions

1. Lay on the trampoline bed, (stomach down) and assume the correct Stomach Drop position: legs together and straight, elbows point outward, head slightly raised. *Do not rise up on your forearms.*

2. Practice going from a Seat Drop into the Hands and Knees Drop then into the Stomach Drop position using the No-Bounce Method. Your seat, hands and knees and stomach should all land on the same spot.

51

3. Do progression 2 with a low bounce before the Seat Drop, Hands and Knees Drop into a Stomach Drop.

4. Do a Stomach Drop using the No-Bounce Method. Start low and slightly hunched over. You can finish this progression in either the hands and knees position or on your feet. Remember that your stomach lands on the same spot that your feet used to be on.

5. Once you have mastered progression 4, try the Stomach Drop using a low bounce making sure that your stomach lands on the same spot that your feet used to be on and finish with the Stop Bounce.

Error Detection and Correction Chart

Error	Correction
nose diving	– lower your bounce – tighten your seat, stomach and back muscles so that all parts of your body touch the trampoline bed at the same time – go back to progression 2 – ensure that your stomach is landing where your feet used to be
your legs are hitting the trampoline bed before your upper body	– lower your bounce – hunch forward and lower your shoulders going into the Stomach Drop – tighten up your seat, stomach and back muscles – go back to progression 2
your head is jerking backward in the Stomach Drop position	– keep your shoulders low on the Stomach Drop, do not rise up onto your elbows or forearms – do not let your chin touch the trampoline bed on Stomach Drop – tighten your muscles so that the legs, torso and arms hit the trampoline bed at the same time
unable to get back onto your feet after doing the Stomach Drop	– keep your body tighter throughout the skill – quickly pull your legs under your body after rebounding off your stomach – push off your hands and forearms, then quickly raise your shoulders and head up from the trampoline bed; do not look down, instead focus on the edge of the trampoline
sore lower back	– lower your bounce or go back to the No-Bounce Method – ensure you land with elbows pointing out to the side (see progression 1) – keep shoulders low during Stomach Drop – tighten seat, back and stomach muscles

For a Challenge

Vary the starting position going into the Stomach Drop: Tuck into the Stomach Drop or Pike into the Stomach Drop.

Your body must be horizontal or very close to horizontal when doing the Tuck or Pike position before the Stomach Drop.

Try some of the following combinations:

Stomach Drop into a Seat Drop

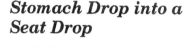

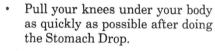

- Pull your knees under your body as quickly as possible after doing the Stomach Drop.

Land both the Stomach Drop and the Seat Drop in the same spot; do not travel forward or backward on the trampoline bed.

Seat Drop into a Stomach Drop

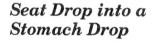

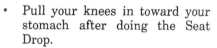

- Pull your knees in toward your stomach after doing the Seat Drop.
- Keep your shoulders low.

Try to do the Seat Drop and the Stomach Drop in the same spot on your trampoline bed; do not travel forward or backward.

Beginner Routines

The following routines will provide a challenge for beginners and reemphasize basic skills for more advanced trampolinists. Ideally, the skills listed for each routine should be performed without additional bounces in between unless indicated. Begin your routine by taking four or five Basic Bounces.

Beginner Routine 1

1. Tuck Jump to feet
2. Pike Jump to feet
3. Straddle Jump to feet
4. Stop Bounce

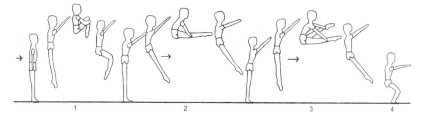

Stay in the centre of the trampoline throughout each routine.

Beginner Routine 2

1. Seat Drop to feet
2. Tuck Jump to feet
3. Seat Drop into
4. Stomach Drop to feet
5. Stop Bounce

Stay in the centre of the trampoline throughout each routine.

Beginner Routine 3

1. Seat Drop into
2. Hands and Knees Drop into
3. Stomach Drop to feet
4. Full Turn to feet
5. Stop Bounce

Stay in the centre of the trampoline throughout each routine.

Beginner Routine 4

1. Stomach Drop into
2. Seat Drop to feet
3. Half Turn Straddle Jump to feet
4. Half Turn Seat Drop to feet
5. Stop Bounce

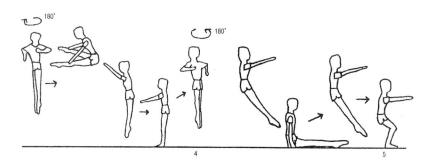

Stay in the centre of the trampoline throughout each routine.

INTERMEDIATE SKILLS & COMBINATIONS

"TO PREPARE TO DO A QUAD-TWISTING FLIPPUS,
LIFT YOUR ARMS UP HIGH OVER YOUR HEAD
AND PULL YOUR KNEES TOWARD YOUR CHEST."
DO YOU WANT ME TO READ IT AGAIN STEVE?

Back Drop

The Back Drop is performed by going from your feet to your back then rebounding back up to your feet. The landing position in the Back Drop is very important: your arms and legs point upward and your chin must be tucked in toward your chest.

Prerequisites

Seat Drop, Stomach Drop

Key Points

* Always start and finish the skill in the centre of the trampoline.

* Keep your chin tucked in so that the back of your head does not touch the trampoline bed.

* Land with your arms in front of your body.

* Keep your hips bent at a 60° angle to the bed in the Back Drop position.

Your back should land on the same spot that your feet used to be on.

Progressions

1. Lay down in the Back Drop position to familiarize yourself with how you will be landing: arms and legs pointing upward, chin tucked in toward the chest and hips bent at a 60° angle to the bed. If you are having difficulty keeping your legs up, bend at the knees but still maintain a 60° angle at the hips.

2. Starting in the Back Drop position, bounce on your back by bringing your knees and elbows

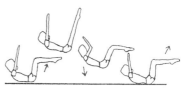

toward your chest then extending the legs and arms up and outward. This is a difficult lead-up skill to master so don't be discouraged if you are unable to perform it immediately.

It is important that you practice bouncing on your back for a number of reasons:

- This simulates how you will land in a Back Drop.
- This progression strengthens the muscles necessary to perform the Back Drop.
- This will help you to develop the coordination necessary for doing a Back Drop.

Note: Place a large piece of foam rubber in the middle of your trampoline bed for progressions 3, 4 and 5. The extra padding will soften your landing and make learning the Back Drop easier and safer.

3. Hold a ball or rolled up t-shirt in front of your body and slightly above horizontal with your arms straight. Squat down so that you are close to the trampoline bed and in one smooth motion, kick one foot up toward the object and land in the Back Drop position.

Once you are able to successfully kick one foot up and land on your back, try kicking both feet up at the same time and land in the Back Drop position.

4. Repeat progression 3, gradually moving from a squat position to an upright position. Do not worry about getting back up to your feet at this point, finish in the Back Drop position for now.

5. Once you are able to do a Back Drop starting from an upright position and finishing on your back, try going from your feet to your back then back up to your feet. To do this, land in the proper Back Drop position with your arms and feet pointing upward, as your body starts to rebound off the trampoline bed, quickly and forcefully snap your legs down and reach forward with your arms.

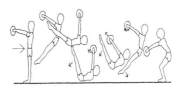

Remember to land in the proper Back Drop position and *wait until your body starts to rebound* upward before you snap your legs downward.

6. Try progression 5 using the No-Bounce Method and without the protective padding on your trampoline bed.

7. Try progression 5 with a small bounce then gradually add additional height to your bounces as you begin to feel more comfortable with the skill. Always finish with the Stop Bounce.

Error Detection and Correction Chart

Error	Correction
unable to land in the Back Drop position landing on your tail bone or lower back instead of on your shoulder blades/upper back	– go back to progressions 1, 2 and 3 until you feel comfortable landing on your back – keep your arms in front of your body and at chest height throughout the Back Drop, do not drop your arms down to your sides or behind your body – kick your legs up higher going into the Back Drop
your head is hitting the trampoline bed	– keep your neck muscles tight throughout the skill with your chin tucked in toward your chest – keep your arms slightly above horizontal and close together, this will help protect your head and neck
landing on the back of your neck instead of your shoulder blades/upper back	– go back to progressions 1 and 2 do not let your hips go past a 60° angle to the bed in the Back Drop position
having difficulty getting back onto your feet after doing the Back Drop	– reach forward with your arms when rebounding off your back to your feet – your back should land where your feet used to be – as your body begins to rebound off the trampoline bed, quickly and forcefully snap your legs downward and reach forward with your arms; your body should rise in a slightly arced motion

For a Challenge

Try the following combinations using the Back Drop:

Back Drop into a Hands and Knees Drop

- Bend the knees slightly after rebounding out of the Back Drop before going into the Hands and Knees Drop.

- Snap the legs down hard coming out of the Back Drop.

- Try to do both the Back Drop and the Hands and Knees Drop on the same spot.

Back Drop into a Stomach Drop

Follow the same key points outlined for the Back Drop into a Hands and Knees Drop, except end in a Stomach Drop.

Cradle

The Cradle combines the Back Drop with the Half Turn. The trampolinist begins by doing a Back Drop, rebounds off the trampoline bed and goes into an upright Half Turn, the legs are then quickly pulled under and the trampolinist goes into a second Back Drop before rebounding back up to the feet. The trampolinist will begin facing in one direction and finish facing in the opposite direction for the Cradle.

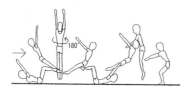

Prerequisites

Back Drop, Swivel Hips

Key Points

- Always start and finish the skill in the centre of the trampoline.
- Pick a focal point and look hard and fast for this point to initiate the Half Turn.
- A solid Back Drop with good form is essential!

Progressions

1. Back Drop Half Turn to feet. Use the No-Bounce Method going into the Back Drop and pick a focal point behind you to look for. Keep your muscles tight so that all parts of your body turn at the same time.

   Remember to do a late Half Turn. Drive your legs down hard and *wait until your body is almost vertical before starting the turn*. A turn that starts too early may

66

cause you to travel toward the edge of the trampoline.

2. Half Turn into a Back Drop is the next step. Begin with the No-Bounce Method. Pivot on your feet then go into a Back Drop. Keep your body tight, legs together and chin tucked in. Once you feel comfortable doing the Half turn into a Back Drop without a bounce, add a low bounce to this progression.

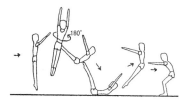

3. Back Drop Half Turn into a Seat Drop. This progression is similar to the Swivel Hips. Pick a focal point behind you to look for coming out of the Back Drop and going into the Half Turn. Pull your knees toward your stomach after the Back Drop, this will increase your rotation making it easier to get into the Seat Drop. Practice this step until you are able to easily move from the Back Drop into the Seat Drop with both your seat and your back landing in the same spot on the trampoline bed.

Remember to land in the proper Seat Drop position with your back straight, hands flat on the trampoline bed by your sides, legs straight and head level.

4. Seat Drop Half Turn into a Back Drop. This progression is also similar to the Swivel Hips. Emphasize a good stretch coming out of the Seat Drop and going into the Half Turn. This will give you more height and control. Upon completing the Half Turn, quickly pull your knees toward your chest and land in the Back Drop position.

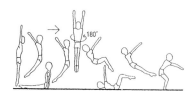

5. Once you have mastered progressions 1 to 4, try the complete skill. Think about snapping the legs down after the first Back Drop to get enough forward rotation, look for a focal point then quickly pull the legs under to get into the second Back Drop.

For a Challenge

Try to do the Cradle with good form: legs straight and together throughout the skill, torso tight and arms straight.

Do more than two Back Drops in your Cradle.

Try the following combinations:

- Cradle into a Stomach Drop
- Stomach Drop into a Cradle
- Swivel Hips into a Cradle

Error Detection and Correction Chart

Error	Correction
unable to complete the Half Turn	– do not wait too long to initiate the Half Turn; as soon as your body rebounds off the trampoline bed and you are approaching vertical, look hard for a focal point behind you – keep your body tighter so that everything twists at the same time and at the same speed – your body should be almost straight in the twist, it is very difficult to twist if you are in a Semi-Piked, or Semi-Tucked position
bouncing off to the side of the trampoline bed	– wait until your body has rebounded off the bed before starting the twist, do not twist too early – ensure that you are landing flat on your back in the first Back Drop with your arms and legs pointing upward – keep your arms shoulder width apart and in front of your body throughout the Cradle
unable to get from the Back Drop Half Turn into the Seat Drop	– when coming out of the Back Drop, quickly and forcefully drive your legs downward and reach forward with your arms – pick a focal point behind you and look hard and fast for that point pull your legs under faster going into the Seat Drop
unable to go from the Back Drop Half Turn into the second Back Drop	– pull your legs under harder and faster – aim for landing with your hips at a 60° angle to the bed and the arms extending upward – go back to progression 3 and practice doing the Back Drop Half Turn into Seat Drop – pull your knees toward your chest after the first Back Drop

Error Detection and Correction Chart (cont.)

Error	Correction
unable to rebound out of the second Back Drop and up to your feet	– your legs may be either too high or too low in the second Back Drop; keep your hips at a 60° angle to the bed in the second Back Drop – after doing a solid second Back Drop with the legs at the correct angle, quickly and forcefully drive the legs downward and reach forward with your arms
landing on your side in the second Back Drop instead of on your back	– do not rush going from the first Back Drop into the second Back Drop; wait for your body to almost reach vertical before twisting – ensure that you complete the Half Turn before going into the second Back Drop; if you are having difficulty completing the Half Turn, go back to progression 3, Back Drop, Half Turn into a Seat Drop – emphasize landing in the correct Back Drop position on both Back Drops

Turntable

The Turntable is a Stomach Drop, Full Turn, Stomach Drop. Throughout this skill, the trampolinist's body is horizontal so that the chest, stomach and hips are pointing toward the trampoline bed on the Full Turn portion of the skill. Beginning with a Stomach Drop, the trampolinist rebounds off the bed and assumes a Semi-Tucked position. The trampolinist then begins to look for a focal point, completes a Full Turn, then extends the legs and torso before going back into the Stomach Drop position.

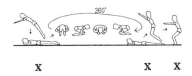

"X" marks the centre of the trampoline

Prerequisites

A solid Stomach Drop

Key Points

* Always start and finish the skill in the centre of the trampoline.

* Your stomach lands on the same spot even during the lead-up skills. Do not travel forward or backward on the trampoline bed.

* Look hard for a focal point to initiate your rotation.

* The proper Stomach Drop position is very important: shoulders low, elbows pointing outward, body straight and tight.

Progressions

1. Bounce on your stomach. Begin this progression using the No-Bounce Method. As your body rises off the trampoline bed, assume a Semi-Tucked position then quickly extend your legs and

71

torso outwards to land in another Stomach Drop. This progression will take a fair bit of co-ordination. Once you are able to perform two consecutive Stomach Drops with all parts of your body touching the trampoline bed at the same time, try for three Stomach Drops, then four and so on.

2. Try to complete a Full Turntable in ¼ segments going from a Stomach Drop ¼ Turn into a Hands and Knees Drop back into a Stomach Drop ¼ Turn, back into a Hands and Knees Drop and so on. Practice this progression using the No-Bounce Method.

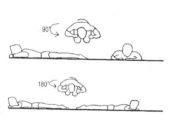

3. Stomach Drop ¼ Turn and into another Stomach Drop. Follow the same steps outlined in progression 1, only this time start looking for a focal point behind you to initiate the rotation.

4. Once you are able to easily perform a Turntable in ¼ segments, try the Turntable in two, half segments.

   Remember to start with a solid Stomach Drop then look hard and fast for a focal point to initiate the rotation.

5. Try a ¾ turntable. Once you are able to do this, try a Full Turntable so that you start and finish the skill facing in the same direction.

For a Challenge

Instead of assuming a Semi-Tucked position on the Turntable, try doing the skill in a Semi-Piked position.

Try rotating in the opposite direction in your Turntable.

Try performing two consecutive Full Turntables with no extra bounce between the two skills.

Error Detection and Correction Chart

Error	Correction
your legs are hitting the trampoline bed before your torso on the Stomach Drop	– review the progressions for a Stomach Drop before trying the Turntable again – lower your shoulders – lower your bounce
having difficulty bouncing on your stomach with or without turning	– concentrate on keeping your body tight and close to the trampoline bed; do not let your legs or shoulders rise too high above the trampoline bed – keep your body tighter, especially your back and seat muscles – assume a Semi-Tucked position in-between each Stomach Drop; do not try to tuck the legs in close to the stomach at first – when you extend out of the Semi-Tucked position, extend out in a smooth and controlled motion, kicking the legs out too hard may cause your back to arch, making it harder to do the Stomach Drop – lower your bounce or go back to the No-Bounce Method before doing the first Stomach Drop
landing on your side instead of your stomach after doing the Turn	– do not pull your shoulder under; keep both shoulders and your hips pointing directly down at the trampoline bed throughout the skill – go back to progression 2 and practice doing solid ¼ Turntables – keep your body tighter so that all parts of your body are twisting at the time and at the same speed – lower your bounce

Airplane

The Airplane is performed by doing a Half Turn into a Stomach Drop. Your stomach should land on the same spot that your feet used to be. Unlike the Half Turntable, where your body is horizontal throughout the turn, in an Airplane the Half Turn is done when the body is in an upright vertical position.

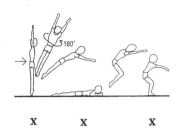

"X" marks the centre of the trampoline

Prerequisites

Stomach Drop into a Back Drop, Half Turn, Full Turn

Key Points

• Always start and finish the skill in the centre of the trampoline.

• Use the No-Bounce Method when first trying the Airplane and the lead up skills for the Airplane.

• Do not rush the Half Turn; a smooth, controlled Half Turn will make performing the Airplane easier than a quick Half Turn.

• Keep your arms above shoulder level in the Half Turn.

Progressions

1. From standing, pivot on your feet (Half Turn), then go into the Stomach Drop. Ensure that your stomach lands where your feet used to be.

2. With one low bounce, do a Half Turn, keeping your shoulders high, then go into a Hands and Knees Drop. Keep your back level in the Hands and Knees Drop.

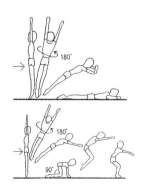

75

3. Using a low bounce, try doing a complete Airplane.

   Remember to do a controlled Half Turn, pick a focal point and have your stomach land where your feet used to be.

For a Challenge

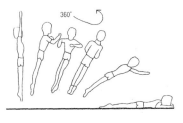

Try turning in the opposite direction for your Airplane.

Try a Full Turn into a Stomach Drop. Your stomach should land where your feet used to be.

Error Detection and Correction Chart

Error	Correction
nose diving into the Stomach Drop	– keep your shoulders higher longer and keep your feet closer to the trampoline bed – slow down; do not rush the Half Turn – your stomach should land where your feet used to be – keep your body tighter and lower your bounce
your legs are hitting the trampoline before your torso on the Stomach Drop	– lift up your feet and lower your shoulders so that all parts of your body hit the trampoline bed at the same time – keep your body tighter – speed up your Half Turn – go back to progression 2 and ensure that your back is flat and you are not sitting back on your heels in the Hands and Knees Drop
not completing the Half Turn	– keep your body tighter – initiate the Half Turn sooner – look for a focal point
going past the Half Turn	– slow down the Half Turn – look for a focal point – keep your arms slightly outstretched to slow down your rotation – initiate the Half Turn later – allow your arms to come up to ear level in the Half Turn
sore back or neck	– keep your body tighter – ensure that all parts of your body are hitting the trampoline bed at the same time – do not go up onto your forearms in the Stomach Drop, point your elbows out to the sides and keep your shoulders low – lower your bounce

Roller

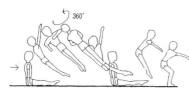

Unlike the Swivel Hips, which uses a vertical, sideways twist, the Roller uses a horizontal, sideways twist. Imagine a pencil rolling down an incline: as the pencil rolls, the eraser stays at one end while the point stays at the other end. This is exactly what happens in a Roller: your torso and feet will remain in virtually the same spot on the trampoline bed throughout the twist and you will begin and end the skill facing in the same direction.

Prerequisites

Seat Drop, Hands and Knees Drop

Key Points

- Always start and finish the skill in the centre of the trampoline.
- Pick a focal point and start and finish the Roller looking at the focal point.
- Keep your legs together and your body tight.
- Start and finish the Roller with solid Seat Drops.

Progressions

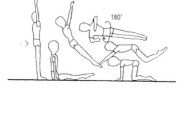

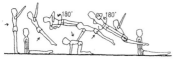

1. Seat Drop to Hands and Knees Drop, (think about rolling sideways). Try this progression using the No-Bounce Method.

2. Carry progression 1 a step further by adding a Seat Drop after the Hands and Knees Drop. Remember to twist in the same direction throughout the skill and do this progression using the No-Bounce Method.

Keep your body as tight as possible to prevent travelling from the centre of the trampoline bed. Ultimately you want to be able to start and finish the skill in the same spot. Ensure that you have complete control throughout this progression before moving onto the next progression.

3. Seat Drop to Seat Drop. Bounce on your seat without going up to your feet. This progression will reinforce the stretched out horizontal phase of the Roller. Try repeating this sequence as many times as possible: Seat Drop stretch to near horizontal, Seat Drop, stretch, Seat Drop, stretch and so on.

4. Roller using the No-Bounce Method. Perform a solid Seat Drop to begin the skill. Stretch your body out coming off the trampoline bed and think of doing a very fast Seat Drop, Hands and Knees Drop, Seat Drop combination. If your body is tight enough and the twist is fast enough, your hands and knees will not touch the bed and you will do the Roller.

5. Try the Roller with a low bounce and finish with the Stop Bounce.

Error Detection and Correction Chart

Error	Correction
doing a vertical (upright) twist instead of a horizontal twist (the skill may look somewhat like the Swivel Hips)	– go back to doing a Roller from a sitting position on the trampoline, roll sideways onto your hands and knees, then continue to roll back over to your seat, (rolling in the same direction), do this progression several times to get your rotational position correct
travelling across the width of the trampoline bed toward the springs	– start the Roller with a solid Seat Drop, (legs straight and together, back straight, hands on the trampoline by your sides), do not try to lunge sideways into the twist; instead, concentrate on keeping your body tight and try to stay in the centre of the trampoline – keep your arms straight and back level on your Hands and Knees Drop in the lead ups for the Roller
unable to complete the full twist	– keep your legs tight and together throughout the skill – keep your torso tight so that all parts of your body twist at the same time – lower your bounce or try the skill again using the No-Bounce Method

For a Challenge

Try a 1½ twisting Roller. You will begin the skill on your seat and finish in the Hands and Knees Drop.

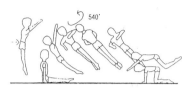

After you have perfected the Roller so that you are able to start and finish in the same spot, try doing two consecutive Rollers: Roller, land in the Seat Drop Position and immediately go into a second Roller before going back to your feet.

Try a double twisting Roller. Make sure you have perfected the 1½ twisting Roller before trying this one!

Intermediate Routines

Intermediate Routine 1

1. Back Drop to feet
2. Pike Jump to feet
3. Airplane to feet
4. Straddle Jump to feet
5. Stop Bounce

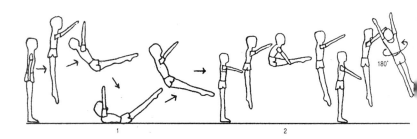

Stay in the centre of the trampoline throughout each routine.

Intermediate Routine 2

1. Full Turntable to feet
2. Tuck Jump to feet
3. Back Drop Half Turn to feet
4. Half Turn to Seat Drop into
5. Half Turn to Back Drop to feet
6. Stop Bounce

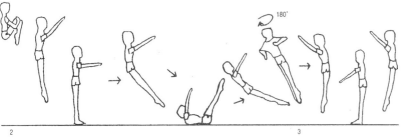

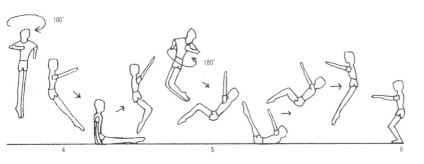

Stay in the centre of the trampoline throughout each routine.

Intermediate Routine 3

1. Roller to feet
2. Straddle Jump to feet
3. Back Drop into
4. Stomach Drop to feet
5. Full Turn to feet
6. Stop Bounce

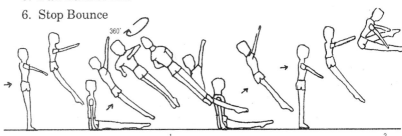

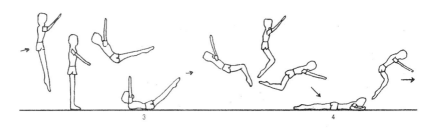

Stay in the centre of the trampoline throughout each routine.

Intermediate Routine 4

1. Cradle to feet
2. Tuck Jump to feet
3. Airplane to feet
4. Roller to feet
5. Full Turntable to feet
6. Stop Bounce

Stay in the centre of the trampoline throughout each routine.

ADVANCED SKILLS
& COMBINATIONS

BUT THAT'S WHAT IT SAYS IN THE BOOK ANGIE,
"TO COMPLETE THE SKILL AT THE ADVANCED LEVEL,
THE FULL-IN-FULL-OUT MUST BE PERFORMED IN A TUTU,
THROUGH A FLAMING HOOP WHILE JUGGLING FOUR BOWLING PINS
IN THE PRESENCE OF A BARKING POODLE"
I CAN'T HELP IT IF THE POODLE WASN'T BARKING.

Cruise

To perform a Cruise, the trampolinist begins with a Stomach Drop, rebounds off the trampoline bed into a vertical position, completes a Half Turn then drops into a second Stomach Drop. The Cruise is similar to the Airplane, which uses a vertical, sideways twist.

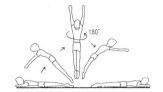

Prerequisites

Airplane

Key Points

- Always start and finish the skill in the centre of the trampoline.
- Quickly push yourself away from the trampoline bed after the first Stomach Drop.
- Do not twist too early, wait until your body is almost vertical before initiating the Half Turn.
- Keep your body tight throughout the skill so that all parts of your body twist at the same time.

Progressions

1. Practice doing a solid Stomach Drop to your feet. Aim for landing straight up and down or slightly leaning backward. Use your forearms and hands to help push your body away from the trampoline bed. Do not go up onto your elbows in the Stomach Drop position. *Always land with your elbows pointing outward.*

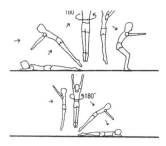

2. Once you are able to quickly rebound out of your Stomach Drop, add a late Half Turn before landing on your feet.

3. Practice the Airplane (Half Turn to Stomach Drop).

4. Put the Stomach Drop, Half Turn and the Airplane together and try the Cruise.

For a Challenge

Try to maintain good form throughout the Cruise: legs straight and together, torso tight and straight.

Try doing more than two Stomach Drops in the Cruise.

Reverse the direction of your twist.

Error Detection and Correction Chart

Error	Correction
landing hunched over on the Stomach Drop Half Turn to feet	– quickly drive your shoulders up and back after doing the Stomach Drop – think about *squeezing* your seat muscles – keep your head level throughout the turn; do not allow your chin to drop down
unable to complete the Half Turn	– keep your body tighter – once your body is vertical, look hard and fast for a focal point behind you to help initiate the twist
nose diving into the second Stomach Drop	– lower your bounce – keep your head and shoulders higher for a longer period of time
legs are hitting the trampoline bed before your torso on the second Stomach Drop	– keep your feet close to the trampoline bed during the twist – lower your shoulders sooner going into the second Stomach Drop – *squeeze* your seat muscles and think about piking slightly to compensate for the possible arch in your back
landing on your side on the second Stomach Drop	– look harder for a focal point once your body is vertical to initiate a faster turn – ensure that both shoulders are pointing down going into the second Stomach Drop – tighten up the muscles in your back, seat and sides – lower your bounce – go back to progressions 2 and 3

Cat Twist

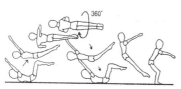

Like the Roller (see "Intermediate Skills & Combinations)," the Cat Twist uses a horizontal, sideways twist. You will begin this skill on your back, complete a full twist and finish on your back. Throughout the skill, your head will remain in a fixed area and your feet and legs will also remain in a fixed area of the trampoline.

Prerequisites

A solid Back Drop, ability to bounce on your back, Roller

Key Points

- Always start and finish the skill in the centre of the trampoline.

- When doing the Cat Twist, think about keeping your shoulders low and your feet and legs high. Optimally, your hips should be at a 60° angle to the bed.

- Keep your legs together and as straight as possible in the twist, this will make the twisting action much smoother and easier to initiate.

Progressions

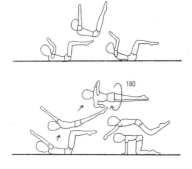

1. Starting in the Back Drop position, try bouncing on your back by bringing your knees toward your chest, then push the legs upward and slightly outward.

2. Back Drop Half Turn into a Hands and Knees Drop with no bounce. Think about twisting sideways to get into the hands and knees position. Keep your back flat on the

Hands and Knees Drop as this will make it easier to go into the second Back Drop as outlined in the next progression.

3. Back Drop Half Turn into a Hands and Knees Drop Half Turn into a Back Drop using the No-Bounce Method. Concentrate on finishing in the proper Back Drop position with your hips at a 60° angle to the bed. Do not allow your legs to drop down going into either Back Drop. Practice this progression gradually adding more and more speed to the twist.

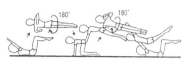

Remember to twist in the same direction throughout this progression and aim for starting and finishing in the centre of the trampoline bed.

4. Once you are able to start and finish progression 3 near the centre of the trampoline bed, try the complete skill without touching down on your hands and knees. Keep your body tight throughout the twist and remember to start and finish the skill in the proper Back Drop Position. Do not go from your back up to your feet on the second Back Drop. *Finish on your back with your hips at a 60° angle.*

5. Add a low bounce to your Cat Twist and instead of finishing on your back rebound back up to your feet after the second Back Drop by driving the legs downward and reaching forward with your arms. Do not bring the legs down too early when trying to get back to your feet. *Wait until your body starts to rebound off the trampo-*

line after the second Back Drop then drive your feet down and your torso and shoulders up.

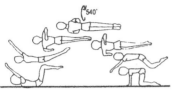

1½ twisting Cat Twist

For a Challenge

Try 1½ twists in your Cat Twist. You will start in a Back Drop and finish on your hands and knees.

Try two Cat Twists in a row: one full twisting Cat Twist to your back then immediately go into a second full twisting Cat Twist before rebounding back to your feet. Aim for landing in the centre of the trampoline bed on both Back Drops.

Try a double twisting Cat Twist. Make sure that you have mastered the 1½ twisting Cat Twist before trying this one!

Error Detection and Correction Chart

Error	Correction
unable to go from the Back Drop into the Hands and Knees Drop	– your legs may be either too high or too low, land with your hips at a 60° angle to the bed – do not drive the legs downward after the first Back Drop, instead keep your legs pointing upward – go back to progression 2
having difficulty going from the Hands and Knees Drop into the second Back Drop	– do not sit back on your heels in the Hands and Knees Drop, maintain a 90° angle behind your knees – keep your body tight so that all parts are twisting at the same time – finish the Back Drop with your hips at a 60° angle to the bed and your arms pointing upward
landing on your side instead of your back in the second Back Drop	– keep your body tighter – think about finishing in a solid Back Drop Position with your arms reaching upward
unable to get back to your feet after doing the second Back Drop	– your legs may be either too high or too low; keep your hips at a 60° angle to the bed in the Back Drops and as your body starts to rebound off the trampoline bed on the second Back Drop, drive the legs downward and reach forward with the arms
head is being jarred back on the second Back Drop	– keep your chin tucked in toward your chest – do not allow your legs to drop down too early in the second Back Drop
travelling sideways across the trampoline bed instead of starting and finishing in the same spot	– do not start the twist too early after the first Back Drop; wait until your body has started to rebound off the trampoline bed – keep your body tight in the twist with the arms pulled in toward your chest

Corkscrew

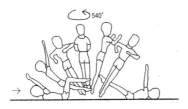

The Corkscrew is a very advanced non-inverted skill and should not be attempted until you have mastered the prerequisites outlined below. A Corkscrew is similar to the Cradle; however, instead of doing a Back Drop, Half Turn, Back Drop, you will be performing a Back Drop, 1½ Turn, Back Drop. You will start facing in one direction and end up facing in the opposite direction.

Prerequisites

Cradle, Cat Twist, 1½ Turn, Double Turn

Key Points

- Always start and finish the skill in the centre of the trampoline.
- Keep your body very tight throughout the Corkscrew with the legs straight and together during the twist.
- Do not rush through the progressions; master each progression before moving onto the next.
- Start and finish in the proper Back Drop position with arms and legs held in an upright position.

Progressions

1. Practice the Cradle with a fast, stretched out Half Turn that passes through vertical.

2. Back Drop Full Turn to feet. Do this progression with a late, fast twist. To speed up your twist, quickly *wrap* your arms in toward your chest with the outside arm

96

pulling across, (if you twist to your right, pull your left arm across and toward your chest). Aim for landing in an upright position or slightly leaning forward. Avoid landing leaning backward.

3. Back Drop 1½ Turn to feet. Use the same arm motion to speed up the twist as outlined in progression 2. Remember to look for a focal point.

4. Full Turn into a Back Drop. Start from standing and lean back going into the Full Turn. Try to land in the proper Back Drop position with your arms in front and straight, legs straight and together and hips at a 60° angle.

5. 1½ Turn to Back Drop. Start from standing, lean forward before pushing off the bed and doing a 1½ Turn into the Back Drop position.

6. Back Drop with a low bounce into a 1½ Turn into a Seat Drop.

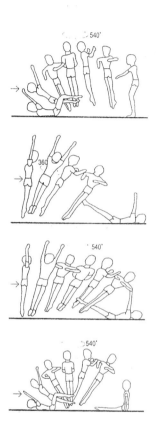

7. Once you have mastered progressions 1 to 6, try the entire skill: Back Drop into a 1½ Turn into a Back Drop. Perform a solid Back Drop, drive your legs down and allow your torso to quickly rise off the bed, complete 1½ twists before quickly pulling your legs under to land in the second Back Drop.

Error Detection and Correction Chart

Error	Correction
unable to land on your feet in the Back Drop Full Turn to feet falling backward on the landing in the Back Drop Full Turn to feet	– drive the legs down harder after rebounding off the trampoline bed on the first Back Drop – keep your arms in front of your body
travelling toward the edge of the trampoline bed	– do not initiate the twist too early; wait until your body has rebounded off the trampoline bed and you are almost vertical – after rebounding off the bed, quickly pull your arms in toward your chest; keep the arms at chest level
unable to complete the 1½ Turn to your feet (stopping at a Full Turn or 1¼ turn)	– practise doing just the 1½ Turn, starting and finishing on your feet – pull your outside arm across your body to initiate a faster twist (if you twist towards the left, pull your right arm across your body); keep the arms at chest level – keep your body tighter – pick a focal point
landing on your side instead of your back on the second Back Drop	– go back to progression 6, (Back Drop 1½ Turn into a Seat Drop) and ensure that you are completing the 1½ Turn before attempting the Corkscrew again – ensure that your feet and arms are pointing upward on the second Back Drop
unable to get into the second Back Drop (doing a Seat Drop or "tail bone drop" instead)	– pull your feet under faster after completing the 1½ Turn – aim for landing with the hips at a 60° angle to the bed with the arms pointing upwards – bend your knees slightly and pull your knees toward your chest before going into the second Back Drop

For a Challenge

Try the Corkscrew with good form:
legs together and straight, body tight,
etc.

Twist in the opposite direction on your
Corkscrew.

Pull-Over

To perform the Pull-Over, the trampolinist begins by doing a Back Drop. Instead of driving the feet back down toward the bed (in the opposite direction), the trampolinist drives the legs backward over the head *after the body starts to rebound off the bed.* This skill will take you upside down and *it is therefore imperative for safety that you have mastered the prerequisites.*

Prerequisites

A solid Back Drop, Cradle, Cat Twist

Key Points

* Always start and finish the skill in the centre of the trampoline.
* Initiate the backward rotation by quickly driving your legs over your head and down toward the trampoline bed.
* After rebounding off your back, bend your knees and assume a Semi-Tucked position; this will speed up your backward rotation.
* Always perform a solid Back Drop before going into the Pull-Over: arms close together and stretched upward, hips at a 60° angle to the bed and chin tucked in toward the chest.

Progressions

1. Practice bouncing on your back. Initiate the bounce by bringing your knees close to your chest then extend the legs upward and outward.

2. From a low bounce, do a Back Drop; as your body rises off the trampoline bed, bend your knees slightly before coming back down onto your back.

3. From a low bounce, do a solid Back Drop; as your body rises off the trampoline bed, *quickly snap your legs over your head* (knees slightly bent) and drive your feet back down toward the trampoline bed.

For a Challenge

Try doing a Pull-Over into a Seat Drop or a Pull-Over into a Back Drop. Aim for starting and finishing in the same spot.

Try doing your Pull-Over with straight legs. To generate enough rotation, assume a deep piked position with your legs very close to your chest.

Error Detection and Correction Chart

Error	Correction
rotation is stopping or slowing down when the trampolinist is upside down unable to initiate enough rotation to complete the skill and finish on your feet	– after rebounding out of the Back Drop, pull your knees in toward your chest much faster and quickly drive your feet over your head and down toward the trampoline bed – do not throw your head backward; keep your chin tucked in toward your chest throughout the skill – keep your knees bent and fairly close to your chest after rebounding out of the Back Drop
twisting sideways	– go back to progression 1 and practice bouncing on your back until you feel more comfortable with this position
touching down with your hands when you are upside down	– do not wait too long after rebounding off the trampoline to drive your feet over your head and back down toward the trampoline bed
travelling too far backwards not starting and finishing the skill in the same spot on the trampoline	– think about not only driving your legs over your head and back down toward the trampoline bed, but also think about driving your feet toward the spot where your back used to be – pull your knees in closer to your chest

Front Flip

The Front Flip is an inverted skill whereby the trampolinist performs a complete forward rotation starting and finishing on the feet. The Front Flip can be done in the Tuck or Pike position. The Tuck position is the easiest position to use when learning the Front Flip. Because the Front Flip is a *very* advanced skill, be sure to master all necessary prerequisites and progressions outlined.

Prerequisites

Full Turntable, Cradle, Cat Twist, solid Tuck and Pike Jumps

Key Points

- Always start and finish the skill in the centre of the trampoline.

- Perform the Stop Bounce after doing the Front Flip.

- Be sure to follow the step-by-step progressions for the Front Flip. You may have already attempted a Front Flip; however, to do this skill with good technique and to avoid travelling too far across the trampoline bed, follow the progressions!

- The tighter the tuck, the faster the rotation. Always place one hand on each shin and pull your knees in close to your chest.

- Bring the arms down narrow and straight from ear level before assuming the Tuck position; this will give you more lift and help initiate the rotation.

103

Progressions

1. Forward roll without bouncing. Place your legs shoulder width apart, bend the knees slightly and place your hands on the trampoline bed. Continue by tucking the head under and far enough back toward your legs that your body rolls forward. As your body begins to roll, grab your shins and pull your knees close to your chest, keeping your knees slightly apart.

2. Repeat progression 1, this time adding a quick push off the trampoline bed so that you have some height going into the forward roll. Aim for starting and finishing in the centre of the trampoline bed.

   Remember to keep your knees apart and pulled in toward your chest. Ideally you should be landing on your back or on your seat in a Tuck Position.

   Your head, neck and upper back should not be touching the trampoline bed. If you find that you are landing on the back of your neck or on your head, go back to progression 1 and try doing a faster forward roll with the chin tucked in toward your chest.

   Do not move onto progression 3 until you can continually land on your seat in a Tuck position.

3. Now try a Hands and Knees Drop into a Front Flip. Land on your seat with the knees slightly apart. This may be a difficult step for

some trampolinists but keep in mind: it is an important progression! By doing your Front Flip from the Hands and Knees Drop, you will achieve the following:

- Reinforce fast rotation in the Flip.
- Prevent excessive travelling in the Flip.
- Reinforce good technique.

Using a low bounce, go into the Hands and Knees Drop (look forward and focus on the edge of the trampoline). As your body starts to rebound, drive your arms down and your hips up. As your body starts to rotate, follow through with the arms by grabbing onto your shins and pulling the knees close to your chest.

Remember to keep your knees apart!

You can start by landing on your seat. Once you are able to consistently land on your seat, try landing on your feet.

This progression will take a fair bit of practice to master. Optimally, you want to finish on your feet without travelling more than two feet (½ metre) forward on the trampoline bed before moving onto progression 4.

4. Once you have mastered progressions 1 to 3, try doing the Front Flip from your feet using the No-Bounce Method. Start with your arms straight and slightly in front of your ears. Forcefully drive your arms down through the centre and

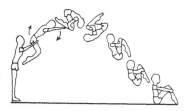

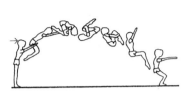

your hips up over your head.

Go from landing in a "cannon ball" or Semi-Tucked position to landing in a squat position and finally an upright position. Do the Stop Bounce as soon as you land your Front Flip.

5. Repeat progression 4, add three or four low bounces before doing the Front Flip. Keep in mind:

• You should not travel more than two or three feet forward.

• Always begin the Front Flip with your arms raised up to ear level.

• Finish the Front Flip with a Stop Bounce.

If you start to travel forward or you are having difficulty landing the Front Flip, go back to progression 3.

Error Detection and Correction Chart

Error	Correction
hitting your face on your knees	– keep your knees and feet shoulder width apart throughout the Front Flip and on the lead ups for the Front Flip
very slow rotation and unable to get onto your seat or feet	– the tighter the tuck, the faster the rotation; pull your knees in close to your chest with one hand on each shin for the tucked Front Flip quickly and forcefully drive your arms downward from ear level to your shins – keep the chin tucked in after leaving the trampoline bed
over-rotating the Front Flip and landing on your hands and knees or falling forward on the landing	– open up (stretch out your legs and straighten your torso) a bit sooner so that you are ready for the landing – do a Stop Bounce with your arms no lower than chest height as soon as your feet touch the trampoline bed
hitting your head on the trampoline bed on the Hands and Knees Drop into a Front Flip performing a very low Front Flip that is rotating very quickly (possibly rotating out of control)	– keep your head level until your body has left the trampoline bed; dropping the chin toward the chest too early on the Front Flip will cause you to rotate very quickly, however, this will also cut off most of your height – wait for your body to rebound off the bed before dropping the chin toward your chest – keep your arms as straight as possible when going from ear level to your shins
falling backward after landing the Front Flip	– generate more rotation by holding the Tuck (or Pike) Position longer – ensure that your knees are close to your chest in the Tuck Position with one hand on each shin

Error	Correction
falling backward after landing the Front Flip	– do not allow your arms to pass behind your head before going into the Front Flip; always start with your arms slightly in front of your ears – drive the arms down forcefully through the centre; do not allow the arms to go out toward your sides going into the Front Flip

For a Challenge

Try doing a Front Flip in the Pike position.

Keep in mind the following key points:

- Start and finish the skill in the centre of the trampoline.

- Drive the arms down much harder for a Front Flip in the Pike position.

- Try to get your chest as close to your legs as possible.

- Bend your knees when you come in for the landing on the Front Flip in Pike position and end with a Stop Bounce.

Advanced Routines

Advanced Routine 1

1. Straddle Jump to feet
2. Airplane to feet
3. Pull-Over to feet
4. Tuck Jump to feet
5. Back Drop into
6. Full Turntable to feet
7. Stop Bounce

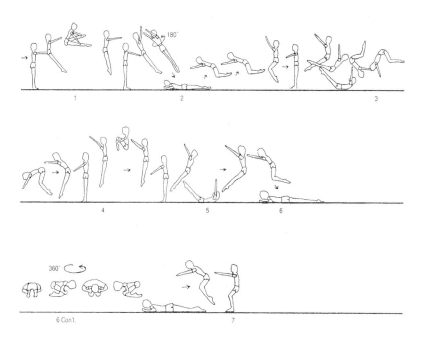

Stay in the centre of the trampoline throughout each routine.

Advanced Routine 2

1. Roller to feet
2. Cat Twist to feet
3. Straddle Jump to feet
4. Airplane to feet
5. Swivel Hips to feet
6. Cradle to feet
7. Stop Bounce

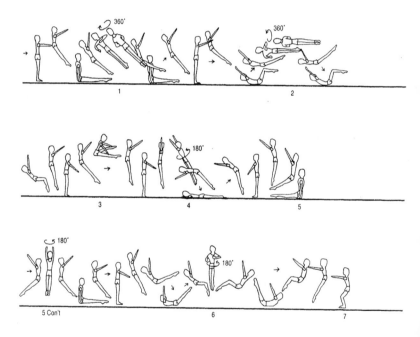

Stay in the centre of the trampoline throughout each routine.

Advanced Routine 3

1. Corkscrew to feet
2. Pike Jump to feet
3. Cruise to feet
4. Straddle Jump to feet
5. Roller to feet
6. Stomach Drop to feet
7. Stop Bounce

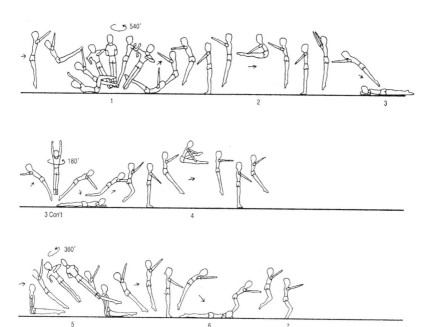

Stay in the centre of the trampoline throughout each routine.

111

Advanced Routine 4

1. Straddle Jump to feet
2. Full Turn to feet
3. Roller into
4. Stomach Drop into
5. Cat Twist to feet
6. Front Flip to feet
7. Stop Bounce

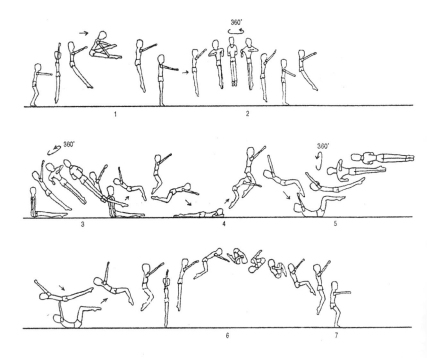

Stay in the centre of the trampoline throughout each routine.

Glossary

60°Angle

the optimal angle between the back of your legs and the trampoline bed in a Back Drop

90° Angle

the optimal angle behind your knees when you are in the Hands and Knees Drop Position

AIRPLANE

an intermediate level skill whereby the trampolinist performs a vertical Half Turn before going into a Stomach Drop

ARCH

a body position whereby the back is swayed and the stomach sticks out; this position should be avoided

BACK FLIP

an inverted skill whereby the trampolinist starts the skill on his feet, performs one backward rotation on the transverse axis and finishes on his feet; Back Flips should not be performed on a backyard trampoline

BASIC BOUNCE

a fundamental skill that is used to gain height and momentum

BED

the part of the trampoline that is used to bounce on

CAT TWIST

an advanced skill whereby the trampolinist performs a Back Drop into a horizontal Full Turn before going into a second Back Drop

CORKSCREW

an advanced skill whereby the trampolinist performs a Back Drop then completes 1½ Turns in a vertical position before going into a second Back Drop

CRADLE

an intermediate skill whereby the trampolinist performs a Back Drop into a vertical Half Turn followed by a second Back Drop

CRUISE

an advanced skill whereby the trampolinist performs a Stomach Drop before going into a vertical Half Turn followed by a second Stomach Drop

DISMOUNT

the way in which a person moves from the apparatus to ground level

ERROR DETECTION AND CORRECTION CHART

a chart designed to identify the various errors made on certain skills and ways in which to correct these errors

FLEXIBILITY

the range of motion in a joint or series of joints

FLYING OFF

an uncontrolled, often dangerous dismount from your trampoline to ground level; flying off is not recommended

FOCAL POINT

a designated spot on your trampoline that you look for to either initiate or stop rotation

FRONT FLIP

an inverted skill whereby the trampolinist starts on her feet and performs one complete forward rotation before landing on her feet again

FULL TURN

a 360° vertical rotation in which the trampolinist twists to the left or right

HALF TURN

a 180° vertical rotation in which the trampolinist twists to the left or right

HAMSTRING AND CALF STRETCHES

exercises designed to stretch the muscles on the back of your legs below the knees (calf) and the muscles in the back of your legs above your knees (hamstring)

HANDS AND KNEES DROP

a beginner level skill whereby the trampolinist goes from his feet onto his hands and knees, then rebounds back onto his feet

HORIZONTAL

a position whereby your torso is parallel to the trampoline bed

INITIATE

to start or begin a certain movement

INVERTED

an upside-down position whereby the trampolinist's hips pass over his head

KNEE DROPS

a skill that should be avoided! the trampolinist goes from his feet down onto his knees (without the use of his hands), then rebounds back up to his feet

LAYOUT

a body position whereby the trampolinist maintains a straight body, the back is flat, the chest is slightly hollowed and there is no bending at the hips or knees

MOUNT

the way in which the trampolinist moves from ground level onto the apparatus

NECK ROTATIONS

an exercise used to stretch the muscles in your neck

NON-INVERTED

an upright position whereby the hips do not go above the trampolinist's head

NO-BOUNCE METHOD

a method of learning new skills whereby the skill is performed from a standstill

PIKE JUMP

a beginner level skill whereby the trampolinist extends the legs forward and reaches for his toes while in the air; the trampolinist starts and finishes this skill on his feet and maintains a straight leg position throughout the jump

PIVOT

a turn on the balls of your feet; your feet do not leave the trampoline bed on the pivot

PULL-OVER

an advanced skill whereby the trampolinist goes into a Back Drop, re-bounds and completes a 270° backward rotation before finishing on the feet

QUAD STRETCHES

an exercise designed to stretch the muscles on the front of your legs above the knees

QUARTER TURN

a 90° vertical rotation in which the trampolinist twists to the left or right

REBOUNDING

bouncing; springing upward

ROLLER

an advanced skill whereby the trampolinist goes from a Seat Drop into a horizontal, 360° rotation to finish on his seat

ROTATION

sideways, forward or backward movement around an imaginary axis

ROUTINE

a series of skills which are performed consecutively without additional bounces taken in between each skill

SEAT DROP

a beginner skill whereby the trampolinist goes from his feet onto his seat with the legs outstretched then rebounds back onto his feet

SEMI-PIKED

a position similar to the Pike; the angle at the hips is greater in a Semi-Piked position than in the Pike position

SEMI-TUCKED

a position similar to the Tuck; the angle at the hips is greater in a Semi-Tuck position than in the Tuck position

SPOTTERS

people stationed around the trampoline who are prepared to push the trampolinist back toward the centre of the bed if he should start to lose control and move toward the edge of the trampoline

STOMACH DROP

a beginner skill whereby the trampolinist goes from his feet to his stomach then rebounds back onto his feet

STOP BOUNCE

a very important beginner skill used to stop momentum when the trampolinist comes down onto his feet

STRADDLE JUMP

a beginner skill whereby the trampolinist lifts his legs to a horizontal, straddle position in the air before bringing the legs together to land on the feet

SWIVEL HIPS

a beginner skill whereby the trampolinist performs a Seat Drop, vertical Half Turn, then drops into a second Seat Drop

TO FEET

a trampolining term meaning to go from a skill back onto your feet

TRAVELLING

moving away from the centre of the trampoline bed

TURNTABLE

an intermediate skill whereby the trampolinist does a Stomach Drop, then horizontal 360° rotation before going back into a Stomach Drop

TWIST

a term synonymous with "Turn" whereby the trampolinist rotates sideways

VERTICAL

the trampolinist's body is in an upright position whereby the hips are below the head

WAIVER

a formal document giving permission to participate in an activity

WARM UP

a series of exercises designed to stretch your muscles

Index

119

Printed in Canada by The Prolific Group, Red Deer, Alberta

About the Author

Darlene Traviss owns and operates seven gymnastic clubs in her home province of Alberta, Canada. She teaches gymnastics and trampolining to children and adults, as well as giving technical instruction to teachers and coaches. In the spring and summer Darlene devotes her time to travelling and writing.

Darlene has been actively involved in trampolining since the 1970s, first as a competitor, then as a coach and a judge. After a lengthy career as a competitive gymnast, Darlene went on to compete as a springboard and platform diver and a freestyle skiing aerialist.

Notes

Notes

Notes

126

Notes